HILL COUNTRY REVISITED

HILL COUNTRY REVISITED

By J. ROY WHITE   Introduction by JOE B. FRANTZ

TRINITY UNIVERSITY PRESS   *San Antonio*

©Copyright 1977 by J. Roy White

Library of Congress Catalog Card Number 77-089818
SBN # 911536-70-1
Printed in the United States of America

Printed by Best Printing Company, Inc.

Bound by Custom Bookbinders

Design by William D. Wittliff

For James and Mary Jo

INTRODUCTION

LIZ CARPENTER, lovable, glowering former press secretary for Lady Bird Johnson, called to me in that commanding tone of hers: "Joe, there's an architect in Austin I wish you'd look up. He's good—a good artist, I mean. He's a good architect, too, or President Johnson wouldn't have used him so much. But he's an artist who's too modest about his own work. Maybe you could encourage him to show you some of his sketches."

Since I used to be afraid of Liz, I complied rather quickly for me. With al-arkity, as we used to pronouce "alacrity" back in Weatherford.

Liz turned out to be as accurate as usual. Roy White was shy as well as modest. I liked his sketches, and suggested he ought to do a small book around them. Roy just shook his head and mumbled, "Aw, I can't believe that anyone would seriously be interested in my drawings."

I told him that I was, and that furthermore, I would back up my interest with some work. If he wanted a text, I'd write one.

The result was *Limestone and Log, A Hill Country Sketchbook*, which with the assistance of Bill Wittliff and his Encino Press we published in 1968. That was nine years ago, and, for a distinctly regional book, it has been a success.

Later, when the Driskill Hotel in Austin seemed destined for replacement by a parking lot, I decided to underline my own inclination toward historic preservation by writing an affectionate memoir about that historic edifice. I asked Roy to provide some sketches of both interiors and exteriors, especially some details of the latter. Again Roy took on his most sincere and mournful look: "Oh, Joe, you can't want me to help on this?"

I did, and we produced a second small book together, which again happily stays in print and keeps the publisher forwarding modest royalties. I know that it's fashionable to say that there are things you'd rather have than money, but I discount such statements as so much pious lip-service. But not with Roy. I do truly believe that if I had to choose between giving up working with Roy White or foregoing royalties, I'd surrender the latter. While I appreciate my annual check, my true pleasure comes from Roy's yearly telephone call and his obvious amazement that anyone would appreciate his work well enough to pay money to purchase it. Although he is a bit older than I, I feel toward him like a doting parent who has discovered in his bright child areas of strength and enjoyment that neither the child nor the world hitherto knew existed.

Now I've never had the least sympathy for feigned modesty. If you have critical facility and you're pretty good, you ought to be able to assay your strengths about as well as any outsider. But Roy's modesty is not false. It's as real as the stone houses he delineates with his pen and brush. I suspect that deep down he knows that he is pretty good, but he can't quite master the wonderment that someone else thinks he's pretty good, too. His is not a hang-dog depreciation of his talents; he just can't quite believe . . .

When we were putting together *Limestone and Log*, Roy came to me. "Joe, I'd feel better if I put in a word of explanation of what I tried to do at the end of the book. Would you mind? Do you suppose I could get away with it?" I assured him that we had no way to know unless he tried it.

The result almost embarrassed me. I had expected a dry-as-dust architect's account of measurements and details and architectural periods. Instead, I read a piece of prose that was eloquent and sincere, that indeed made me wonder whether I dared let my own little prose sketches stand alongside his afterword. But I decided that I hadn't entered this collaboration to compete. I had no doubt where the quality lay. Roy had told it all in a couple of pages, and he had shown a poetic flair in the summation.

So now this gentle Louisiana native is moving along to another rung. He is going to write the sketches and draw the sketches—do the whole book by himself. But still he can't quite let go of his friends. As he said to me, "You and Bill Wittliff have had a hand in both my efforts thus far. I just couldn't publish another book unless you wrote something and Bill did the design." He doesn't need us, though I hope that he keeps thinking he does, because I like to hang around him.

Where Roy White is concerned, of two things I feel certain. When in the generations ahead, our progeny wonders what the Hill Country portion of Texas looked like in the latter twentieth century, they'll find nowhere a more faithful evocation of the country than in Roy White's sketches. He combines an architect's precision with an artist's eye.

The other certainty is personal. I started out with a reticent stranger a decade ago. Somewhere in there I found not a collaborator, but a friend for life. Of that I am truly proud.

JOE B. FRANTZ
The Ides of June 1977

ACKNOWLEDGMENTS

To do another book similar to *Limestone and Log* published by Encino Press, 1968, has been a challenge ever since its publication. Like the man who climbed the mountain because it was there, I wanted to accept the challenge. But twenty-four pencil drawings were *not* there. They were off somewhere in time and distance, and it has taken some mighty pushing and shoving to get me back to work on them. Two years ago Patsy and Marshall Steves started pushing and shoving in admirable fashion or I would still be thinking and not doing. When I learned that Trinity Press might consider a few color reproductions, I finally made that hesitant beginning. I want to express sincere appreciation to the Steves for their continual encouragement which changed hesitancy to enthusiasm.

Joe Nicholson and Lois Boyd, Trinity Press, couldn't know that they would be up against someone who thought he could write as well as draw. Thanks to them both for being patient with me.

I also want to especially thank Bill Wittliff of Encino Press, who designed and published *Limestone and Log,* and who agreed to design this book. My equally fervent thanks go to Joe Frantz for writing the Introduction for me. I could not have faced another book without the *Limestone and Log* team being a part of it.

The drawings of the LBJ Ranch House and of the Johnson Birthplace were used through the gracious consent of Mrs. Lyndon B. Johnson and of the Lyndon Baines

Johnson Library. I want to express my particular appreciation to Mrs. Johnson and to Gary Yarrington of the Library for the loan of these sketches. The Dietz Bakery, Hensel House, and Travis Peak School are drawings owned respectively by Fredolin Kaderli of Fredericksburg and by Mary Jane Murchison Smith and Mrs. E. A. Murchison, Jr. of Austin. All were gracious in allowing them to be reproduced. Drawings other than those listed in this paragraph are the property of the author.

Maude Folmar Ramsey, my "friend and severest critic," gave me the encouragement I needed in the completion of each of the drawings. Without her knowledge of values, technique, and "feel" for good work, I would have been lost.

There were numerous other folks who assisted and cooperated in many ways: Jean I. Black who loaned me Otto Lindig's book and who could keep me entranced with many of Otto's tall tales; Ethel Matthews Harkins whose history of the Hensel family was invaluable; Josephine Prowse Edwards who gave further information about the Hensels; Mrs. Hondo Crouch for her Fredericksburg awareness; Mr. Joe Weinheimer who told me a bit of history of Rocky Hill School; Mrs. Elise Kowert of the Fredericksburg *Standard*; Mildred P. Mayhall for her frank and considerate appraisal of my efforts; and my wife, Mary, whose opinions I treasure and respect, who thinks every sketch I do is *"good,"* and who has patiently looked forward to the completion of all of them.

I really don't know how to adequately express my appreciation to all these folks. There couldn't have been a book without their help. Reckon I just say, from the heart, thank you.

J. ROY WHITE
May 1977

CONTENTS

HILL COUNTRY REVISITED

Nine years have passed since the publication of *Limestone and Log,* and I continue to talk about houses and trees and hills and flowers and days gone by; about ever-changing time and weather; about things that you have not noticed before. A tiny cemetery, partly hidden by brush and cedars, suddenly comes to view on a knoll not 200 yards from the highway, with cast iron fence surrounding a few molding tombstones held up by a modicum of upkeep. Or you see for the first time a gnarled and twisted live oak composition; a rare madrone tree, a new patch of flowers, or Spanish goats on a hillside; or a cabin in the distance caught by the sun just for you.

The most tantalizing thing about the hill country is what you do *not* see. What is beyond that hill in the distance? What secrets does this rocky little creek hold as it rushes around the bend? What old farmhouses, barns, stone walls are up that rough and dusty road?

Again, I only scratch the surface of the hill country charms, its habitations, its remembrances, its ways of life too dear to be forgotten, because no book on the hill country can ever be complete. There are subtle differences each time a person travels through it, as if the country has a way of putting on a new face for those who care to see; a new face with a change in the weather, a change in the season, a change in the time of day.

For those who love foggy, misty days, the hills take on a mystic quality, standing out like stage pieces, in soft profiles one behind the other, ever approaching, ever receding. Or, on a brittle cold and bright winter day, the hills stand chased of color by the dry chill, and the fields, the trees, the hillsides are a canvas of dull and shiny grays, and of tones of browns and tans and darks, and bare branches are silhouetted against the sky and against the warm gray-greens of the live oaks and the black-greens and bronzes of the cedars.

There are days just as bare and harsh in midsummer, when heat waves shimmer and strange little mirage pools keep appearing on the road ahead, then disappearing to leave you wanting for a real lake or a small stream or anything to help forget the dryness. It is then that the hills and valleys seem to blend together in flat planes and become part of a landscape seared by the sun, the heat, and the wind. On a return trip the same day, the clouds can begin to gather and you become part of a hill country "happening," with black storm clouds rolling across the hills and lightning flashes and thunder and torrential rain, and you experience not just the sight of the hill country in the storm but the hearing and the feeling, too, if you will only bare your face to the rain.

And springtime! What a beautiful time in the hills, from the beginning when the peach orchard branches are red and full with the promise of good fruit, and the redbuds and the buck-eye stand against bare hills in unbelievable pinks and magentas. Bright lemon greens tinge the tips of the cedar elm trees, and the Spanish oaks seem to be in bloom with their fresh new leaf buds of color. By the time the trees get all dressed up, here come bluebonnets and paintbrush and primroses and wild verbena and coreopsis waves and winecups and gaillardia and horsemint heralding the summer, and fields of "snow-on-the-mountain" and yellow daisies and gay-feathers and goldenrod and purple asters and Maximilian sunflowers. And all of a sudden it is autumn.

The hill country in the fall is another time of color—when the sumac and the red and Spanish oaks are dressed in muted opulence. When a lone chinaberry tree stands out like yellow gold and the elm trees are turning in their finest burnished copper and the waves of prairie willow flaunt their white silver plumes along the roadsides. The regal Maximilian sunflower nods in all its splendor in stately acceptance of your delight in its beauty. The post oaks are warm umber and vandyke brown, rich and soft in their proclamations heralding the beginnings of winter. Autumn colors in the hill country epitomize the ruggedness, the stability, the endurance of the hills in understated colorings—a moderate statement of the fulfillment of growth.

To me, fall is the most beautiful of the hill country seasons. Or rather, sometimes I think so, and then I remember morning drives in any season with the sun low and the shadows defining so expertly the hill contours, the ranch homes and barns, the early sun warm and promising. Or I remember late afternoons with the unbelievable, indefinable richness of a setting sun; with magnificent sunsets that seem more a part of the whole land from east to west. And I wonder, what is the most beautiful time?

What is the most beautiful time? No matter how many times any road is traveled, there is always a time of beauty. Maybe it is only a spot of color, a passing mood, an object not noticed before. Sometimes there is almost too much for one man to grasp and hold to and remember, but I know that the beauty of the hill country, of any country, belongs to me to try to hold forever—the color, the hills, the wind in the trees—all mine to be treasured and to remember. Such beauty is also yours, something we own together, to share, to bind us with some strange and indefinable bond—such beauty that almost hurts with a stab of reality that says it cannot be held in your heart for a lifetime.

In the Afterword of *Limestone and Log* I wrote ". . . the old buildings deserve a sort of respect and attention—and they all seem to beg for just a little compassion, just a little understanding from all of us—proud and happy when cared for, rugged and brave in their slow neglect and isolation."

I have begun to realize during the past years that the most evident changes in the hills have been in those buildings themselves. Maybe their hope for compassion is reaching folks. So many of the subjects sketched for *Limestone and Log* have been restored or are being restored, and many more are being loved and cared for. Maybe this would have happened anyway, but I like to think *Limestone and Log* had something to do with it.

Presuming somewhat on the patience and interest of the reader, it pleasures me to report briefly on the condition of some of those buildings.

xvii

THE PAISANO LOG CABIN on the Dobie Ranch is well cared for by the University of Texas in its rejuvenation as a typical early Texas log cabin. There is definite hope that it will be completely restored.

THE MILLER CREEK HOUSE has been happily rescued by its owners and sits proudly for all to view from U.S. 290 on the banks of Miller Creek.

THE STONE BUILDINGS near Johnson City are now the "Old Farm" area, owned and operated by the National Park Service as a part of the Lyndon B. Johnson Historical Site. Considerable research by the Park Service has resulted in a meticulous reconstruction and restoration of the buildings to achieve the exact form of the original structures.

THE BOYHOOD HOME in Johnson City is also a part of the LBJ Historical Site and was restored to its original appearance as it was when President Johnson was a boy. The sketch of the late restoration of the home is included in this book.

THE ROUND MOUNTAIN STABLE AND LODGE has been purchased and is being personally restored by its new owners in a most careful and deliberate manner.

THE POST OFFICES at Sandy, Hye, and Albert are being well cared for. Hye especially is always resplendent with its old world cornices refreshed every year or so with red, green and white paint.

FRITZ LINDIG HOUSE, vacant when *Limestone and Log* was published, has been bought and has become again a typical hill country ranch home. The Erwin Lindig house across the road to Albert stands just as it was, tirelessly waiting for something to happen.

HODGES HOUSE AND BARN is vacant and owned by the Texas Parks and Wildlife Department as a part of the further expansion of the Lyndon B. Johnson State Park. The Department has completed all restoration on the Sauer homestead and barns in the Park, re-creating an active farm group typical for each of its three periods of time. Hopefully a similar use can be found for the Hodges place.

THE FRUIT STAND on Rocky Creek has gone the way of many roadside shops and has moved into a box-like structure that must better satisfy the owners' needs. The hill country has lost a spot of roadside color.

THE DANZ HOUSE, now known by its new owners as another "Sauer" house, has been faithfully restored in all respects with additional rooms and porches added to seem a part of the earlier 1890 construction.

BLUMENTHAL now boasts a highway sign noting the location of the old community and of the present buildings which have been successfully restored. An antique shop occupies the old Blumenthal store just next door, and the porches and gingerbread on the two-story building have been rebuilt. All shines brightly with fresh white paint.

LUCKENBACH is quite another story, having been

"discovered" and developed as an area attraction in such a successfully outrageous manner that it has lost some of the original secluded charm to the joys of rock bands, Chili Cook-offs, Dirt-dauber Festivals and no telling what else. It is at least still there and well maintained.

SOMEONE began a valiant restoration effort on the Fredericksburg fachverk house a few years ago with new shingles and rebuilt stonework, but nothing more has happened. It waits patiently on time, money, and, I suppose, inclination to return to its former state.

I DROVE through Sisterdale not long ago and was happy to see that the little Sisterdale School no longer serves as a hay-barn. There are new shutters, front door, and paint, and a new fence around the whole area.

THE FREDERICKSBURG "SHOP" looks just as it did 15 years ago when I first noticed it—a beautifully proportioned little building still crying for help. Most of the other buildings are continuing to be used or lived in—the typical Sunday House, the Nebgen and Nuñez homes, Albert School, Lewis Ranch, Blumenthal Farmhouse. But the little "Albert Road Log House" is gone. I like to think that it had to wait too long, then forlornly crumbled away in fragments and returned to the earth from which it came, alone.

Whether or not such efforts as this have encouraged the revitalization of hill country places, this effort continues just the same, and *Hill Country Revisited* presents another batch of drawings intended again to portray hill country scenes. These buildings then are what I've found up that dusty road, over that hill, or down that rocky creek.

HILL COUNTRY REVISITED

VISITOR'S CENTER

THE VISITOR'S CENTER doesn't rate the designation of an old hill country structure, but its design was influenced by enough of the houses around Stonewall to have realized a bit of the "feel" of the hill country and its rooms contain so much history that it has found a place in this book. It was completed in 1968 and forms the nucleus of the Lyndon B. Johnson State Park established and operated by the Parks and Wildlife Department of the State of Texas.

3

TRINITY LUTHERAN CHURCH

A LUTHERAN MISSION was established in the Albert community in 1902. Not long afterward the first church building was dedicated on the banks of the Pedernales, a few miles east of Stonewall. The present structure came later and is an excellent example of Gothic architecture adapted to the materials and construction methods of the times. Its church spire, its soft gray pressed tin walls in brick patterns, its gleaming white woodwork can be seen from a distance, and it seems to have become a symbol of the people of the neighborhood who "treasure the traditions of simplicity of life, of thrift and of honesty, handed down to them by their parents and grandparents, the founders of this community." (*Stonewall Centennial*, a booklet published by The Stonewall Centennial History Committee, The *Radio Post*, Com. Printers, Fredericksburg, n.d.)

BIRTHPLACE OF LYNDON B. JOHNSON

THE BIRTHPLACE HOUSE, originally built in the 1890's, is a reconstruction based meticulously on conditions and structural findings on the site and by recollections of the family and neighbors. Most helpful were photographs received from the White House archives. The work was completed during the first year of the President's term of office, and the house is now a part of the Lyndon B. Johnson Historic Site which includes the original ranch and ranch house, the Junction School, the boyhood home, and the "Old Farm" in Johnson City.

BOYHOOD HOME OF LYNDON B. JOHNSON

THE BOYHOOD HOME of President Johnson has been subjected to two restorations, once when he was Vice-President and later by the National Park Service. The earlier work was mainly a repair project and no restoration to the 1912–1920 period was attempted. A few partitions were removed, new asphalt shingles installed, the old screened porch glassed in, and fresh paint applied. After the National Park Service acquired the home, through careful and deliberate research the house was restored precisely as it was when Johnson was a boy, complete with a new shingle roof, screened porch, and rooms as they originally were. Even the old picket fence was rebuilt around the house.

THE LBJ RANCH HOUSE

THE ORIGINAL two-story LBJ Ranch House was built around 1895 and has been growing ever since. One and two-story additions were made through the years until it reached its general form when bought by Senator Johnson in 1951. From that time until 1967 there were changes galore. A west wing was added; the dining room, kitchen, and service rooms were enlarged; additional bedrooms were added on both floors. Through all its stages of growth, the house remains a comfortable and homelike place, so proper and agreeable for a Texas ranchman and his wife who were also President and First Lady of the United States of America.

FRIDAY MOUNTAIN

The Old Johnson Institute almost looks twenty-five years younger since my son was last there as a Friday Mountain camper in 1952. Although not too much has changed except for a new fence and a new screened porch, it seems all too refreshed and shiny to be as picturesque as it was then. The picture of "Old Bristletop" still hangs in its accustomed place, though, and the tales that would be told about the fierce-looking old gentleman would scare the be-jeepers out of the new boys, especially when they would learn that his final resting place was right there on the Friday Mountain property. It must have taken courage in the 1850's to establish a school in the rugged hills so far from any town. It probably also took courage to establish a summer camp for a bunch of unpredictable boys in the 1940's, but this most recent career for the old building has been the best thing that ever happened to it—and to the boys who have been a part of it.

13

NEBGEN RANCH BUILDINGS

TO MEASURE A DISTANCE, old-timers used to tie a rag around one of the wagon wheels and start counting the revolutions. When they figured they had driven a mile, they set a notched cedar post by the roadside and drove on for another mile, unless they had by that time counted themselves to sleep. The Nebgen Ranch Buildings are five miles from the intersection of Ranch Roads 1320 and 2721 and you won't have to count wheel revolutions. Just drive west over a pleasant and curving country road around the hills and you will see the buildings on a hilltop to the left of the road. There is a gate, of course, but you will not trespass. Drive slowly a bit farther for a spectacular view of the Pedernales valley with a series of "tanks" stepping down the steep hillside in a succession of terraces. This can be a breathtaking sight when the tanks are full of glistening water and the miles of hills and valleys are hazy in the distance. Alfons Nebgen built the first log cabin, still there and adjoining the typical story and a half stone house of a later date. The one-story stone addition with its unusual sloping roof is of a still later time.

FARMHOUSE RUIN

IN SEARCHING for exactly the right kind of stone to build a "typical dog-trot cabin" (of five bedrooms!), a couple discovered this old two-story ruin, fell in love with the fire-colored stone, and had it carefully taken down, stone by stone, and moved many miles to a site near one of the Colorado River lakes. The resulting new house has become a delightful translation of a forsaken old home into a new and happy place. The date on the gable stone said 1893. Of all the material in the moving process that could have been damaged beyond repair, that had to be the one. The ruin was desolate and beautiful in its stark reminder of what a fire can do in the country.

16

HOUSE THAT HAD IT ALL

THIS HOUSE had a sampling of almost every sort of construction known to builders in the nineteenth century: log construction; fachverk (half-timber) with both stone and brick; plaster; a stone lean-to; boards and battens; mill-run horizontal siding; corrugated iron, tin roof, wood shingles, and even a Victorian gingerbread bracket and post trying to hold up what was left of the front porch roof. The house was on the property where the "Farmhouse Ruin" was located. It was indeed a hopeless case and must surely by this time have gone the way of all unwanted houses.

HENSEL HOUSE

MILES AWAY from familiar U.S. 290 hill country, the northwest part of Travis County is also very much a hill country area, settled during a later time by the same sort of hardy pioneers who came to New Braunfels and Fredericksburg. Among those who came to Travis County was Herman Ludwig Hensel, arriving in Texas by way of Cape Horn and the California gold mines. He evidently came with enough gold to buy eighty acres on Cow Creek, build a log cabin, raise a family of nine children, and establish the farming community of Travis Peak, which he named after the highest hill in Travis County. The Hensel House drawing was done from an old photograph taken not long after the fine stone house that he built was finished in 1878. Its present appearance, except for a screened porch across the front, is essentially the same.

The Hensel House at Travis

TRAVIS PEAK SCHOOL

THE TRAVIS PEAK SCHOOL remains just a one-room stone building with a few benches inside, its kind of schooling long ago gone. This sketch imagines it as it might have been. Back in the early days, Herman Ludwig Hensel gave the property to the school system. Minna Hensel, his daughter-in-law, who still lives in the Hensel House, has given the schoolhouse and the Hensel acreage to the Church of Christ through the Hensel Memorial Foundation. The school will someday be restored. The schoolhouse is near the Hensel place, and all six of the Hensel girls and the three Hensel boys learned their ABC's within shouting distance of home, and also under the watchful eye of their father who was chairman of the School Trustees, Postmaster, and Election Judge until he died.

The Schoolhouse at Travis Peak, 1890

RANCH ROAD BARN AND TANKS

EXPLORING with friends somewhere on a ranch road between Bee Caves and Henly, we found this abandoned barn with a windmill and two beautifully constructed stone tanks for watering the stock. The friends allowed that the big tank was for the big cows and horses, and the little tank was for the little cows and horses. Or just as unreasonably, maybe the rancher was thinking that he would create an interesting composition for a picture someday. Which I hope he did.

24

J Roy White
1977

J Roy White
1975

Old Farm House

OLD FARMHOUSE

"OLD FARMHOUSE" has no name; it almost has no particular place, because I don't know whether I could find it again. Look down an unpaved road somewhere in the Cave Creek area northeast of Fredericksburg—or look in a dozen other places in Central Texas—and you can see so many more just like it. I made a quick sketch of the house in this particularly dilapidated condition and finished it at home much later. Maybe by this time someone has brought it back to life.

HEINRICH LINDIG HOUSES

HEINRICH LINDIG and his wife Amanda came from Germany to Texas in 1867. In 1868 Heinrich built this log cabin, probably the oldest building in the Stonewall community. Two years and two children later, the larger house was built. Otto Lindig was born in the "big house." He died not long ago, but not without leaving a heritage to the people of the area; an oral heritage as well as a written one. Otto loved to talk, and the yarns he could tell about the Stonewall community in the early 1900's have become a part of the lore of the countryside. A favorite, told and retold, is about the cows that came to church: on hot summer Sundays all the cows in Stonewall would come and stand in the shade on the west side of the church to keep cool while chewing their cuds and meditating. They must have also come to enjoy the hymns and the preacher, too, because one of the more religious old cows would stick her head through the front door and let out a long and mellifluous "moo-ooo-ooo" right in the middle of the sermon. The preacher, naturally flustered over such a disturbance, would lose his line of thought, his place in the Bible, and his composure, and yell out "Shut up!," and other words in German, then glare out over his congregation and demand in a tremulous voice, "Now where was I?"

HOUSE ON THE OLD CREEK ROAD

THIS OLD HOUSE now serves as a hay storage place on a small farm on Onion Creek, near Dripping Springs. It is past all help now, but when I first saw it, those clothes were flapping on the line and the wind was blowing and the old Ford was in the shed and it was being lived in.

30   It was somebody's home.

BRUEMMER BARN

SOUTH OF BLANCO on the road to San Antonio lies the community of Twin Sisters, proudly displaying a historical marker. Twin Sisters must have been a busy place in times past; there are many old stone and frame buildings in the neighborhood. Travel east on the Little Blanco Road for the picture of a tiny frame church and cemetery on the left. Then, down the road, on the R. W. Bruemmer place, is what I believe must be the largest, most beautiful, and almost spectacular barn in the hill country.

33

THE BAT ROOST

BUILT IN 1918, this Bat Roost is undoubtedly the most unusual structure in the Hill Country and is also surely the only one. Bat Roosts were fairly common in Texas earlier in the century, as well as in other parts of the world. The production of guano was only secondary; the control and eradication of malaria was foremost. Everybody knows that bats like to eat mosquitoes, so why not encourage hordes of bats, eliminate malaria, and sell guano. Until improved medication became a more controlling factor and with a name like "Dr. Campbell's Malaria-Eradicating Guano-Producing Bat Roost," the idea probably worked. In his book, *Bats, Mosquitoes and Dollars*, Dr. Charles A. R. Campbell (San Antonio) says "If some of our brethren, dear readers, pooh-pooh the eradication of malaria by the cultivation of bats, it is simply because they do not understand. . . . It is inconceivable that any man, who understands the great havoc malaria plays, . . . should be so bereft of the milk of human kindness as in any manner to impede this life-saving, health-giving, wealth-producing beneficence . . . " (p. 134).

COMFORT DEPOT

BACK IN 1887, when railroads were beginning to reach out from urban areas to country folks, Comfort became a focal point in the shipment of grain, cotton, and other farm products to San Antonio over the San Antonio and Aransas Pass Railroad. One Mr. Ingenhuett of Comfort had a brewery on Cypress Creek and was doing fine with his beer, said to be as good as the Menger Hotel product in San Antonio. With the coming of the railroad, things sort of fell apart for Mr. Ingenhuett when San Antonio breweries began shipping their ice-cold beer to the thirsty Comforters by train. (*A Hundred Years of Comfort in Texas: A Centennial History* [San Antonio: The Press of the Naylor Co., 1954].) What's left of Comfort Depot is now well preserved as a gathering place for more recent beer lovers, and anyone there who thinks he sees the ghost of an 1887 steam engine behind the depot just must realize he has had too much of Mr. Ingenhuett's beer.

In this drawing at a distance is a glimpse of the *Treue der Union* Monument (Loyalty to the Union), dedicated in 1866 to the memory of the German settlers of the Comfort-Fredericksburg area who lost their lives during the Civil War in the Battle of the Nueces, defending their belief in the solidarity of the Union. The remains of the dead are interred on this site.

WELFARE

DRIVING from Comfort to Boerne on I.H. 10, a highway sign says "Welfare 5 Miles." A place called "Welfare" so close to "Comfort" sounded somewhat strange, so I drove over one day to satisfy my curiosity. The little road went right through—or past—Welfare, and I found out that Welfare must need welfare, or comfort, or something. The old roadbed of the Fredericksburg and Northern Railroad (it went no farther north than Fredericksburg) is still visible, and Welfare must have once been a sizeable community. Now all that remains is a farmhouse in the background and the lonely Welfare Store, that has a sign:

Welcome to Welfare, Texas
CLOSED

SHARNHORST

THE RANCH SHARNHORST with its background of immense granite crags and boulders piled up in tumultuous confusion evokes feelings of a Wagnerian opera, but there are no Valkyries leaping from crag to crag and no Rhein Maidens in the rushing Pedernales. You somehow expect some dark and mysterious meaning for the German surname, but my Fredericksburg friends assure me there is none. The little farmhouse sits in serenity against the chaotic masses of granite. When sold to its present owners, it became a guest house with the hundreds of acres surrounding it turned into a deer preserve. The hardy ranchers who lived there in the past could never have been happier than the people who visited there in later years.

41

ST. BARNABAS CHAPEL

FOR MANY YEARS an Episcopal mission, this little house is now a chapel for the new St. Barnabas Church built in the late 1960's. Drury Blakeley Alexander in *Texas Homes of the Nineteenth Century* (Austin: Published for the Amon Carter Museum of Western Art by The University of Texas Press, 1966) establishes it as the Peter Walter home, dated 1847, and surely one of the first houses in Fredericksburg. One can easily imagine it as one of Seth Eastman's 1847 drawings in the *Seth Eastman Sketchbook.* The low entrance door did not prevent tall Texans from coming to worship, but a too-tall Texan, though not an Episcopalian, might have found it desirable to genuflect anyway when entering.

DIETZ BAKERY

DIETZ BAKERY was a millinery and dressmaking shop and a boarding house before it became a bakery and long before it was transformed into its present state as a branch office of a savings and loan corporation based in Austin. The building was constructed by George Wahrmund in about 1876, but there is evidence that the one-story part was built at an earlier date. Mrs. Wahrmund must have enjoyed a successful "Millinary and Dressmaking" store. According to an advertisment in an 1888 Fredericksburg newspaper, "I have the Famous D. W. Moody's dress patterns for sale, and I will give instructions on the use of this system. Dresses may be custom-made . . . to please every lady, and offered at the lowest prices." The "esteemed Ladies" of the community were invited to inspect her "most complete stock for the summer season at the Trimmings and High Fashion Store." When the building became a bakery, its rooms were filled with the aroma of the baking of delicious German breads and pastries, an art that continues today as an enticement to visit Fredericksburg. And now the building houses a savings and loan association, with no more frilly dresses, no more *apfel strudel*, but with a caring for people who appreciate the thoughtful return to its original appearance by

its new owners.

ROCKY HILL SCHOOL

IN FULL VIEW from U.S. Highway 290 and seventy-five years away from present-day school architecture, Rocky Hill has remained one of the few country schoolhouses left in the state. This year, 1977, during its 90th year of existence, it has closed its doors for good and has become a part of the Fredericksburg Independent School District. The school was established on land given by the owners of the property in the 1880's. The cornerstone says that the one-room stone building was not built until 1902; the one-room frame addition was constructed in 1915. Maybe "team teaching" and "open classrooms" are not so new after all. For seventy-five years this two-room schoolhouse has been filled with boys and girls of all ages, learning and becoming good citizens of the Rocky Hill and Grapetown communities.

The future of the building is hopefully good; under the terms of the gift of the property, the land reverts to the original owners when the school is abandoned, but only if the building is removed. Surely some proper use can be found for such a historical structure.

CORDES HOUSE

IN FREDERICKSBURG, its dilapidated porch looking over Town Creek, its backyard occupied by a frame bungalow on the corner of Crockett and Mistletoe Streets, stands another of the forlorn reminders of the last century. It was built by the Cordes family and must be more than a hundred years old, judging from structural and architectural details and condition. It is included in this book not just because it is old and picturesque, but because its destiny is in the hands of someone who truly appreciates its value and will see that it is cared for.

May there be many others who feel the same way about our inheritances from the past.

THE AUTHOR

J. ROY WHITE was born in Crowley, Louisiana, and has made his home in Austin, Texas, since 1924. He received his Bachelor of Science Degree in Architecture from the University of Texas in 1929 and was in architectural practice from 1929 to his retirement in 1975.

Mr. White's watercolors and pencil sketches have been exhibited at Laguna Gloria, the Elisabet Ney Museum, the Winedale Museum, and at the Lyndon Baines Johnson State Park. His drawings have appeared in *Limestone and Log,* of which he was co-author with Joe B. Frantz, and he illustrated the book, *The Driskill Hotel,* by Joe B. Frantz. He was also author of private printings of *The Restoration of the Birthplace of President Lyndon B. Johnson* and *The LBJ Ranch House.*

He is a member of the Board of Directors and past president of the Austin Heritage Society and was on the Board of Directors of the Austin Natural Science Association from 1975–77. He is a member of the American Institute of Architects, Texas Society of Architects, Texas Fine Arts Association, and the National Trust for Historic Preservation. Awards which he has received include Architecture of Merit Awards from the Texas Society of Architects and from the Austin Chapter of the American Institute of Architects, a Bronze Medal from the Beaux Arts Institute of Design, a Citation from the Austin Heritage Society, and a Certificate of Commendation from the American Association of State and Local History.

In this book, Mr. White is not concerned with leading the reader by a map route through the hill country nor in rendering exact replicas of the scenes before him. He has taken a few liberties with the landscapes and told the tales of the region without intensive research. What Mr. White does is to leave something to the imagination of the reader, to tease the eye, and perhaps to persuade someone to seek out similar sights on a drive through the country that Mr. White obviously loves so much.

BIBLIOGRAPHY

Books and Booklets

Alexander, Blakeley Drury. *Texas Homes of the Nineteenth Century.* Austin: Published for the Amon Carter Museum of Western Art by The University of Texas Press, 1966.

Johnson, Rebekah Baines. *A Family Album.* New York: McGraw-Hill, c. 1965.

Jutson, Mary Carolyn Hollers. *Alfred Giles: An English Architect in Texas and Mexico.* San Antonio: Trinity University Press, 1972.

Lindig, Otto. *100 Years: Historical Recollections of Gillespie County.* Stonewall, Texas, 1970.

Ransleben, Guido Ernst. *A Hundred Years of Comfort in Texas: A Centennial History.* San Antonio: The Press of the Naylor Company, 1954.

The Story of Fredericksburg. Booklet compiled and edited by Walter F. Edwards. Fredericksburg Chamber of Commerce, 1969.

Stonewall Centennial. Booklet. The Stonewall Centennial History Committee, The *Radio Post*, Com. Printers, Fredericksburg, n.d.

Newspapers

The *Fredericksburg Radio Post.*
The *Fredericksburg Standard.*